We Get You!

30 DAYS
30 WOMEN
30 STORIES
One God

Sandra—
May God surprise you!

REDEMPTION
PRESS

Cristi

We Get You!

30 DAYS
30 WOMEN
30 STORIES
One God

with
Carol Kent
Tammy Whitehurst
Lori Boruff

Athena Dean Holtz
managing editor

Published by Redemption Press, PO Box 427, Enumclaw, WA 98022.

Toll-Free (844) 2REDEEM (273-3336)

Redemption Press is honored to present this title in partnership with the author. The views expressed or implied in this work are those of the author. Redemption Press provides our imprint seal representing design excellence, creative content, and high-quality production.

ISBN 13: 978-1-951350-18-5 (Paperback)
978-1-951350-19-2 (ePub)
Library of Congress Catalog Card Number: 2023906223

Blessed assurance, Jesus is mine
Oh, what a foretaste of glory divine . . .
This is my story; this is my song.
praising my Savior all the day the long.

—"Blessed Assurance,"
Fanny Crosby, public domain

Contents

Preface

Thirty days, thirty women, thirty stories leading to hope. The stories found on these pages were written because we all have a story to share.

As you meet the women on these pages, you will discover how they encountered divine grace somewhere in the middle of their story. It is that place where the shift begins and hope enters the storyline.

You will see yourself among these pages as you encounter real stories that require real faith. Embrace this next thirty days with confidence, knowing you will find someone who has walked this path you now tread.

This devotional is about me.

This devotional is about us.

This devotional is about you.

But most of all this devotional is about Jesus! He is the one who changes the narrative of our stories. Our lives do not always turn out the way we had planned, yet when we look back, we see grace extended by the hand of our beloved Father, and this leads us to hope!

Being confident of this,
that he who began a good work in you
will carry it on to completion
until the day of Christ Jesus.

~ Philippians 1:6 NIV

Dedication

To ALL the attendees of the
Christian Communicators Conference
who stood tall with a call from the Lord
to be speakers and writers.
As CCC sisters, may we always make our stage
an altar as we share the good news of Jesus
with our audiences, no matter how big or small.

How beautiful ... are the feet of those
who bring good news ...
~ Isaiah 52:7 NIV

Introduction

This thirty-day devotional is a compilation of the women who attended the Christian Communicators Conference in Fort Worth, Texas, August 2022.

These women all have a passion to point people to Jesus through their stories told from the stage, from their writing, and across the table.

As you read the stories, allow the truths from these pages to enter the depths of your soul so you may experience all Jesus has for you in *your* story.

You are not alone, my friend. We have walked this journey and found Christ to be the reason for hope in our lives. We bring you our stories as encouragement within your own—and can't wait to see how God meets you in the everyday places of your life.

Each day you will discover:

A verse of encouragement to guide the reading.

A personal or biblical story you can enter.

A truth and application making the story relevant to you.

Then you will be given the opportunity to respond to what you have read in five simple steps.

- Purpose: Recognize the purpose of the teaching and how it relates to your current circumstance.

- Practice: Journal your thoughts to make this truth personal.
- Prayer: Use this prayer prompt as a catalyst to begin your own prayer.
- Promise: Remember the promise. Write it down or take a snapshot with your phone to keep it in front of you throughout your day.

We would love to hear from you about what God is doing within you as you spend the next thirty days with us. Contact us by sending an email to *info@redemption-press.com*. When you send us a note, be sure to include how you found this devotional and how we can pray for you. We will share this with the authors of this book. Just as they hope to encourage you, your words will encourage them!

Our Prayer for You

Father God,
We pray collectively for the women
who read these words.
May each one find a place to enter into our experiences
so they may see You alone at work
within each storyline.
Use these moments to surround her
with Your presence
And draw her into Your grace.
May You be glorified through us
as we hand over our stories for Your use.
Because of Jesus,
Amen.

1

Grace

Be kind and compassionate to one another,
forgiving each other, just as in Christ God forgave you.
—Ephesians 4:32 NIV

God's grace is always on purpose.

Not long ago, a girlfriend shared with me that her husband was struggling with an addiction to pornography. I wanted to weep at the beauty of her words. "I was really angry when he first told me about the porn. But after a day of crying and praying, I realized we were married—a team—and we needed to face this head on. He has work and counseling to do, but he's not doing it alone. I'm right there with him because we are one, and I carry his burdens like he carries mine."

That's grace. And I'm happy to say their marriage flourished under it.

Jesus never had harsh words for hurting people, only for the arrogant. His compassion for the brokenhearted was never ending. What a powerful example to follow.

Purpose

Grace can be hard, but the examples Christ modeled
for us show us holy grace is never an accident. It
always has a purpose. And we need to be purposeful
with our grace as well.

Practice

What is testing your ability to offer grace?
Is there any infraction against you so great that God
can't heal it? Let God use the opportunity
to show his power.

Prayer

Lord, my strength is in you. Hold me close
when I am weak so your love can shine
through the darkness.

Promise

But he said to me, "My grace is sufficient for you, for
my power is made perfect in weakness." Therefore, I
will boast all the more gladly about my weaknesses, so
that Christ's power may rest on me.

—2 Corinthians 12:9 NIV

~ Robin Luftig

2

Celebration

But the righteous are glad;
they rejoice before God and celebrate with joy.
—Psalm 68:3 CSB

God invites us into a life of celebration.

Music, singing, dancing! It sounds like a party, right? Oh boy, it was! Right there on the banks of the Red Sea, Miriam led the women in a celebration that I imagine the Israelites had not experienced for over 400 years. Freedom from the Egyptians at last!

The women danced while Miriam played the tambourine. Moses led the people in a triumphant song to recognize God's miraculous defeat of Pharoah and his army. God had shown up in a big way and freed his people to lead them into a new life with him.

Though plagues, death, and destruction were still fresh in their minds and hearts, the Israelites celebrated. They danced with joy. They shouted; they sang. A celebration occurred as their enemies were being swept away in front of their very eyes.

Life does not need to be perfect to celebrate. Life won't be perfect. Life won't stop. Busyness and pain will always be with us, but God is good. God is always working. God is always present. God is always worthy of a celebration.

Our broken world needs more joy and celebration. We need those things to remind us we have a good God and He is in control. Finding ways to celebrate each day, both big and small, will restore our hope, help us experience an abundant life, and show gratitude to the One who is worthy of our praise and celebration.

Purpose

Celebration allows us to look beyond where we are
and to rejoice in the One with us.

Practice

When was the last time you recognized the Lord's
goodness
and heartily celebrated?

Prayer

Lord, help us to look beyond our circumstances
and celebrate you with joy and gratitude.

Promise

The Christian always has reason to celebrate.
When we fail, celebrate His grace.
When we are blessed, celebrate His mercy.
When others reject us, celebrate His love.[1]

—Larry Crabb

~ Joy Wendling

---

1 Larry Crabb, *The Pressure's Off: Breaking Free from Rules and Performance*
(Colorado: Crown Publishing Group, 2012), 151.

3

Hope

"For I know the plans I have for you," declares the Lord,
"plans to prosper you and not to harm you,
plans to give you hope and a future."
—Jeremiah 29:11 NIV

Gratitude can fill our hearts even when our hope for God's promises is lacking.

Oh, how I longed to be married! I desired the peace and joy I saw in older Christian couples, but it wasn't until I took my eyes off my wants and focused on what I could do for others that God could bring the right man into my life.

I almost lost hope as I prayed for so long for this one request to be answered. Then suddenly, it happened! God gave me the relationship of my dreams.

Now married, I am grateful for my season of singleness as God used that time to help me understand myself, grow my faith, and serve my church. This season led me to be a stronger Christian for my husband and future family.

During this time when I felt a godly relationship was hopeless, I didn't understand the truths God wanted me to learn. Trials teach us invaluable lessons, but only if we let God work in our life in His way and in His timing.

God has a good plan, and we have always been a part of it. His plan leads us to focus on serving people as selflessly as Christ did. Then He will work out the details of our life for our good.

Purpose

Gratitude is the best mindset. Trust God is working and have hope for whatever promise you have yet to receive.

Practice

Where is your hope lacking? How can you thank God for what He has done? Then how can you bring the hope of God's promises to others as you serve them?

Prayer

Lord, help me trust your promises each day with unfailing hope for the future and gratitude for your faithfulness, regardless of what I do not see happening right now.

Promise

But those who hope in the Lord will renew their strength. They will soar on wings like eagles; they will run and not grow weary, they will walk and not be faint.

—Isaiah 40:31 NIV

~ Mary Alice Miner

4

Resilience

*But the God of all grace, who hath called us
unto his eternal glory by Christ Jesus,
after that you have suffered a while, make you perfect,
stablish, strengthen, settle you.*

—1 Peter 5:10 KJV

Resilience is the audacity to bounce back after adversity. Sometimes life can hit you like a ton of bricks. I felt like everything that could happen to me did, all at once. It began with an increase of tuition at daycare. Then all four tires on my truck needed to be replaced, and the refrigerator stopped working. Between my husband and kids we had several trips to the hospital within a two-month timeframe.

Life was indeed getting the upper hand, and I was for sure in the valley.

Have you ever felt that way? Have you ever questioned how long your storm would last? Have you contemplated throwing up your hands and saying, "I'm done! I've had enough. I can't do this anymore. It's just too much. I'm over it."

Thanks be to God; storms don't last forever. Joy does come in the morning with a brighter day ahead. The trying of our faith works patience. But most of all, we find hope during our trials, strength in our weariness, and power in our weakness.

We will endure tribulation, but we must be of good cheer, because Christ has overcome the world. We will suffer, but it's only for a little while. We will get back up again.

Purpose

The next time you go through a storm in your life, remember you can handle it~with God. You will come out stronger, better, and wiser than you were before the test began.

Practice

What storms are you battling at this moment that have tested your faith or caused you frustration, doubt, or fear?

Prayer

Lord, I am believing in you to calm my storm. Give me the strength to get through every test and the resilience to overcome adversity.

Promise

The righteous cry out, and the Lord hears them; he delivers them from all their troubles.

—Psalm 34:17 NIV

~ Na'Kedra Rodgers

5

Behold, I am doing a new thing; now it springs forth,
do you not perceive it? I will make a way in the wilderness
and rivers in the desert.

—Isaiah 43:19 ESV

Are you dizzy from the cycle of defeat?
"Weight?" the registration clerk queried.
"300."

Her laughter suddenly pierced my ears and my heart. My husband and I stood there expressionless as I reiterated, "300."

In labor for our first child, I was in no mood to deal with a naïve clerk. But the sting from that encounter lingered for years.

How could I allow myself to reach this point? When would the cycle stop?

I prayed for God to give me stronger willpower and skinnier thighs. I even had vision boards including pictures of fit women I longed to resemble. How often I awoke in the morning with fierce determination that today was the day I would get it right.

The issue didn't lie in *what* but in *why*. I was trying to remedy my spiritual depravity with an earthly band-aid, until finally I pleaded, "Lord, what am I missing? I can't do this on my own."

Thus began the restoration process.

When we acknowledge our inadequacy and God's sufficiency, grace steps in. His abundance satisfies our deepest longings and fills our every need. In His loving-kindness God will reveal our idols and ask for surrender.

Ephesians 4:22–24 (ESV) tells us, "To put off your old self, which belongs to your former manner of life and is corrupt through deceitful desires, and to be renewed in the spirit of your minds, and to put on the new self, created after the likeness of God in true righteousness and holiness."

Purpose

God restores us from the inside out
through His sanctification.

Practice

Is there an area in your life
that needs restoration?

Prayer

Father God, reveal to me today
what needs to be restored, and take
your rightful place in my heart.

Promise

By trying to grab fulfillment everywhere,
we find it nowhere.[2]

—Elisabeth Elliot

~ *Christina England*

---

2   Elisabeth Elliott, *Passion and Purity* (Revell Books, a division of Baker Publishing Group © 2021), 19.

6

I have swept away your offenses like a cloud,
your sins like the morning mist.
Return to me, for I have redeemed you.

—Isaiah 44:22 NIV

*H*ave you ever had that sinking "morning after" feeling of deep sorrow and regret?

Have you ever experienced a loss so deep . . . so tragic . . that you awoke the next day still in disbelief?

Have you ever felt despair in a situation with no hope for a good resolution, much less a happy ending?

I certainly have. And so did Peter.

Saturday.

Jesus was dead.

Peter was grieving. The choking cloud of shame robbed him of a complete breath.

Far too many times in my own life, betrayal of my Savior makes me want to hide my face from him, but Psalm 139 reminds me there is nowhere I can go where He isn't there. He knows my thoughts before they become formed words. My actions never surprise him nor catch him off guard. He knew before he knitted me in my mother's womb that, by forsaking Him, I choose my own way. He knew the crushing weight of shame I would bear because of my destructive choices.

I have often wondered what Peter did with the heaviness of his "morning after" actions.

He had betrayed the one who had promised eternal life.

In the moments of suffocating shame, did he simply hide away, tearing his robes in despair?

Was he isolated and alone, dark, and hopeless, with no inclination of the difference the dawning of the third day would bring?

Dare he even pray?

Then came the morning.

Jesus was alive!

Not only was Jesus alive, but the words He spoke to Peter in John 21:54–62, "Feed my sheep," resonated purpose in Peter's burdened soul. Peter was redeemed. Forgiven. Restored to fellowship. And so are we.

Purpose

All the grief, shame, and regret
was erased in one heavenly breath.

Practice

Are you weighed down
by the shame of your past?

Prayer

Lord, thank you for my redemption
through the cross.

Promise

There is hope! Run to Jesus.
He died to take away our sin.
He rose again to erase our shame.
You are covered by grace.
And *that* changes everything!

~ Pam Mitchael

7

Called

You did not choose me, but I chose you
and appointed you so that you
might go and bear fruit~fruit that will last~
and so that whatever you ask in my name
the Father will give you.

—John 15:16 NIV

*H*as God called you to do something and you have not put your yes on the table yet?

I remember standing outside the door to the room where I taught *Healing for Our Wounded Heart* to a group of women at Christian Women's Job Corp. I just finished teaching the last class of the semester, and these were my parting words, "God will use your stories if you let Him."

With my hands outstretched in front of me, I said, "So live your lives like this, and say yes to whatever He asks you to do."

The same day, I was introduced to the state consultant for the CWJC. Following a brief conversation, I was asked to speak at the retreat for their executive directors. What could I do but say yes after I had just challenged the women to put their yes on the table.

What has God called you to do? Talk to your neighbor whom you have been too nervous to approach? Or perhaps sing a solo at a large event at church? Our yes opens the door for God to use us to bear fruit.

Purpose

God will use you if you let Him.

Practice

If you feel called by God to do something,
what is holding you back?

Prayer

Father, help me say yes
to what you are calling me to do.

Promise

You were made by God and for God,
and until you understand that,
life will never make sense.[3]

—Rick Warren

~ *Susie Roberts*

---

3 Facebook post, January 4, 2013.

8

Perseverance

I can do all this through him
who gives me strength.
—Philippians 4:13 NIV

Many times, life doesn't turn out like we pictured it would. When this happens and we find ourselves on an unknown path, we have a choice to make about how we will handle our circumstances.

A massive stroke at age twenty-nine caused me to lean into the traits of perseverance, positivity, and faith. I am grateful God blessed me with these traits prior to my stroke because they have carried me through my journey.

I often think of the famous fable of The Tortoise and the Hare when I think of perseverance. The tortoise was slow, like me with a disability after my stroke, but dependable and steady. In the end, he was the one who won the race.

It's often easy to depend on God when things are going well. But when our journey takes a detour and challenges come up, we need to persevere to get through. Even though the picture has changed, God is still right beside us, ready to hold our hand. He desperately wants us to persevere in faith and hope with Him.

Purpose

Our everlasting true hope can only come from our faith in God. Things will go wrong in this world, and daily life is not always easy. When we keep God by our side and take it one steady step at a time, just like the tortoise, we will make it to the finish line.

Practice

What circumstance in your life did not work out as you hoped? How were you able to persevere through the challenges you faced?

Prayer

God, help me face each situation with a strong faith and hope in you, and continue to persevere to live in the plan you have designed for me.

Promise

But those who hope in the Lord will renew their strength. They will soar on wings like eagles; they will run and not grow weary; they will walk and not be faint.

—Isaiah 40:31 NIV

~ Lori Vober

9

Assurance

Let us draw near to God with a sincere heart
and with the full assurance that faith brings.

—Hebrews 10:22 NIV

When we have assurance in God's character, we can grow strong in Him.

David's experience in the wilderness was extremely challenging, yet he had a promise in hand. He would be the next king! There came a point in this story when King Saul, the reigning king, became maniacally jealous of David. The next thing you know, David was on the run for fifteen years in the desert! These are hardly circumstances that signaled his promised throne was around the corner. It must have taken great confidence in God's faithfulness and His character for David to not lose heart.

But David's relationship with God did not start in the desert. It began in a different type of wilderness while tending his father's sheep. There he killed a lion and a bear and found God to be his protector, his provider, and his strength. David deliberately tucked that knowledge away in his heart. He became so steeped in his belief in God's character that later he killed a giant while declaring who his God was!

God's heart is for us to know Him fully. We can then use this understanding to build our faith. This foundation is necessary if we are to have full assurance of our faith in Jesus, His death, and His resurrection.

Challenging circumstances will come. But when we lean on our knowledge of God's character, and let that grow and assure our faith, we can endure and succeed.

Purpose

Dwelling on the richness of God's character
will bring us into assurance of our faith in Christ.

Practice

What circumstance has God brought you through?
What did you learn about His character?
Who is God to you?

Prayer

Lord, open my eyes to the truth of who You are.
Show me Your strong character.
Help me to tuck this truth away in my heart
so my faith in You will grow.

Promise

The Lord is my strength and my shield;
my heart trusts in him and I am helped.

—Psalm 28:7 BSB

~ Cristi Helin

10

Discernment

Let those who are wise understand these things.
Let those with discernment listen carefully.
The paths of the Lord are true and right,
and righteous people live by walking in them.

—Hosea 14:9 NLT

Studying God's Word and listening to the voice of the Holy Spirit gives us discernment, which leads to spiritual guidance and wise decision making.

It was the beginning of the year, and I was struggling with overcommitment. I said yes to too many projects and was having trouble figuring out the difference between "better" and "best" as a Christian leader. It was hard to say no to people I cared about and to kingdom work that I valued~ but I was becoming anxious, exhausted, and unfocused.

A verse I'd memorized as a child came to mind. "Teach me knowledge and good judgment, for I trust your commands" (Ps. 119:66 NIV).

I soon realized that true discernment doesn't just mean distinguishing right from wrong; it means determining the primary from the secondary and the essential from the optional.

As I prayerfully studied Scripture and listened to God's voice, I sensed a quiet calm as I realized saying no to some things~even good things~meant that I had time to say yes to the things God wanted *me* to do.

Instead of uneasiness and fatigue, I experienced joy and peace in following God's leading.

Discernment affects the way we live. It is learning to think the way God thinks~practically and spiritually. As we immerse ourselves in biblical principles, our ability to apply His instruction to our everyday circumstances enables us to make wise choices. We become intentional about listening to the Holy Spirit because His role is to be our teacher and our guide.

As we study the life of Christ, we develop discernment, the ability to recognize the important implications of different situations and courses of action. We cultivate a sense of how things look in God's eyes as the Holy Spirit guides our thoughts and our responses. We make confident decisions and accept responsibilities that fit our spiritual gifts. The result is contentment.

Purpose

When we are uncertain about a course of action,
we can read God's Word, listen to His Spirit,
and discern His will.

Practice

In what area of your life do you need discernment
to make the right choice? What Scripture are you
applying as you seek wisdom?

Prayer

Lord, I commit myself to being a student of the
Word and to listening for Your voice.
Help me make wise choices based on Your truth.

Promise

Whether you turn to the right or to the left,
your ears will hear a voice behind you, saying,
"This is the way; walk in it."

—Isaiah 30:21 NIV

~ *Carol Kent*

11

"Where is your faith?" he asked his disciples.
In fear and amazement, they asked one another,
"Who is this? He commands even the winds and
the water, and they obey him."

—Luke 8:25 NIV

*D*eep-water experiences turn fear into faith and obedience into opportunities.

What did Moses, Jonah, and Peter have in common? They each had a deep-water experience that turned fear into faith and obedience into opportunity.

Moses, along with approximately two million people, stood at the shores of the Red Sea while an entire Egyptian army closed in behind. Fear tempted the Israelites to return to bondage.

Jonah boarded a ship to Tarshish, the opposite direction God told him to go. When a violent storm arose, the crew believed they would die. Jonah knew his disobedience caused the storm and demanded to be tossed into the sea. Man overboard! Jonah's disobedience landed him in the smelly belly of a giant fish.

Peter demonstrated great faith by walking on water toward Jesus. Go, Peter! But his faith faltered when his eyes turned from Jesus to the waves washing over him, and he began to sink.

Like many others in the Bible, these three men had a deep-water experience that turned fear into faith and obedience into opportunities.

Moses obeyed God's instruction to raise his staff and stretch his hand over the sea to divide the waters. Everyone passed safely on dry ground. Jonah cried out to God and then obeyed Him by preaching to the wicked Ninevite people, and God saved them. Peter's fear turned into faith when he reached for Jesus, the only One who could save him.

I found myself in the deep end when my doctor delivered a cancer diagnosis I didn't want to hear. It left me facing impossibilities, running in the opposite direction, and struggling to keep my eyes on Jesus. Yet, through this deep-water experience, my fear turned into faith and obedience into opportunities to witness God's faithfulness and healing power.

Purpose

Deep-water experiences turn fear into faith
and obedience into opportunities.

Practice

Are you struggling to keep your head above water?
Where is your faith?
It is never too late to cry out to God and obey!
He is with you.

Prayer

Lord, my eyes are on You, and I trust You to turn my
fear into faith and obedience into opportunities.

Promise

When you pass through the waters,
I will be with you.

—Isaiah 43:2 NIV

~ Lori Boruff

12

Oh, taste and see that the Lord is good!
Blessed is the man who takes refuge in him!

—Psalm 34:8 ESV

Proclaiming God is good is not the same as believing it with your life.

"God is good all the time; and all the time, God is good." Sound familiar?

Uplifting as that seems, how does a person truly know the goodness of God, especially when life is riddled with heartache?

Betty learned of God's goodness through a life laden with loss. She lost her brother in a drowning accident. Then her husband suffered a heart attack, leaving her alone with three small children. Shortly afterward, she buried both parents. Her daughter-in-law died from an aneurism during childbirth. Both Betty's son and a second wife became ill and passed away. The final blow came when her grandchild was struck and killed by a drunk driver.

Yet Betty will not burden you with tragedies endured but will testify to the goodness of God she has experienced through the difficulties.

The goodness of God is more than a hope-filled catchphrase, but manifests from personal experiences. Beyond a verbal declaration of truth, the Bible invites us into an individual experiment to *taste and see* God's goodness for ourselves.

No doubt we will encounter situations that call the goodness of God into question. The truth of the Bible assures us and invites us to participate in what runs deeper than words on a page.

God is good.

All the time.

Still, you need not take David's word for it or testimonies from friends. Experiment for yourself. Taste of God's goodness and see. Indeed, He is a good God!

Purpose

Experiencing the goodness of God leads to knowing
God is good and not the other way around.

Practice

How can you experience God's goodness
in your current circumstances?

Prayer

Lord, give me courage to taste of your goodness,
experiencing it with my life
and not simply my words.

Promise

God has revealed a thousand things which we shall
never understand, and yet we can know them
by a living, trusting experience.[4]

—Charles Spurgeon

~ *Cheri Strange*

---

4 Charles H. Spurgeon, "The Three What's," The Spurgeon Center, accessed
September 5, 2022, https://www.spurgeon.org/resource-library/sermons/the-
three-whats/#flipbook.

13

Delight

Your words were found, and I ate them.
Your words became a delight to me and the joy
of my heart, for I am called by Your name,
Yahweh God of Hosts.

—Jeremiah 15:16 HCSB

What is the oddest thing you've ever eaten? I'm not brave with food, so the most radical thing for me is adding jelly to a peanut butter sandwich.

However, I am a consumer and connoisseur of words! I love to read, write, and speak *lots* of them!

My favorite *recipe* of words is found in Scripture. It's comprehensive, challenging, and comforting in every morsel. It's filling too, for He is our portion in all things.

I love this version of Jeremiah 15:16 because my name, Kris, means "Christ follower." So I am literally "called by His name." You are too, no matter your name!

Every question can be answered in the Bible as we are reminded to, "Lean not on your own understanding" (Prov. 3:5 NIV). I often say, "Ditto," as Jesus and the Holy Spirit intercede for my lack in what to say, think, or do.

With all the Bible's promises and stories of faith-filled living, I know the satisfaction, delight, and joy that His words give. When we're struggling to find our way, it's a road map. The more we study, the more the path is illuminated and understandable.

Staying close to Him aligns our desires with His. So feast on Scripture! No better entree than God's Word, and no better outcome than delight!

If you need me, I'll be at the *66 Book Cafe*, reading. Come, join me!

Purpose

What you are learning as you taste His goodness
on the written page are great ways to consume the
Word! I'm so thankful we have a written account of
*HIS*tory to pick up anytime we need encouragement!

Practice

What is your favorite way to *digest* God's Word:
memorizing Scripture, listening to Scripture songs,
reading favorite passages, or journaling?

Prayer

Heavenly Father, bind us to your Word as our favorite
meal! Help us see what we put in will come out of
our mouths. May we share with others the joy found
in feasting on Your Word. Your Son is the Word we
treasure and You delight in! Amen.

Promise

Take delight in the Lord, and He will give you
your heart's desires.

—Psalm 37:4 HCSB

~ Kris Howsley King

14

Happiness

The hopes of the godly result in happiness,
but the expectations of the wicked
come to nothing.
—Proverbs 10:28 NLT

I've heard it said, "God is more interested in our holiness than in our happiness."

Jeremiah called himself a man who had seen affliction. Under the rod of God's wrath, he felt as though God was against him. His tribulation and physical adversity made him bitter. Jeremiah felt as though God had walled him in and made his chains heavy. Though he cried for help, God shut out his prayer. Jeremiah claimed his soul was bereft of peace and he had "forgotten what happiness is." His endurance had perished and so had his hope. His soul continually rehearsed his afflictions and was bowed down within him.

But when he made the choice to call to mind the truth about our God, he regained hope. Regardless of his circumstances and the absence of happiness, Jeremiah reminded his soul: "The steadfast love of the Lord never ceases . . . great is your faithfulness. The Lord is my portion, says my soul, therefore I will hope in him."

Life is hard and happiness is fleeting. What we set our minds on—how we remind our souls of the truth of who God is—will determine how we grow spiritually. Will we allow whatever God brings to refine us and sanctify us, leading to holiness? It's a choice only we can make.

Purpose

If there's no emotional bandwidth left,
we can still choose to remember.

Practice

Do you have a situation where it's hard
to hope in Him?

Prayer

Lord, help me remind myself of your faithfulness
even when I'm not happy.

Promise

May the God of hope fill you
with all joy and peace as you trust in him,
so that you may overflow with hope
by the power of the Holy Spirit.

—Romans 15:13 NIV

~ Athena Dean Holtz

15

Endurance

*We celebrate in seasons of suffering because we know
that when we suffer, we develop endurance,
which shapes our characters.
When our characters are refined, we learn
what it means to hope
and anticipate God's goodness.*
—Romans 5:3-4 VOICE

Have you ever thought, *Life's just too hard?*
Counting the times Paul was stoned, imprisoned, or just experienced difficulties makes us wonder how he endured. From his conversion on the road to Damascus, to being beaten and flogged numerous times, pelted with stones, persecuted in many cities, including imprisonment, and finally being

beheaded, his life was one of endurance~ all for the sake of Jesus Christ. Paul's faith allowed him to draw strength from God's Spirit in him.

Paul's life was forever changed when he believed in Jesus as the Messiah. He no longer depended upon himself for wisdom and understanding but on the Spirit of God living in him. He endured without compromising his faith as he focused on eternal joy, because his inner strength was God-given.

In life difficult times come. Tragedy, loss, illnesses, and other problems can make us want to give up. It is easy to become discouraged. It's a relief to know we never face our difficulties alone. We can endure the hard things in life because of Christ in us.

- Feeling as if you're not good enough? God makes us more than enough.
- Feeling as if you're not strong enough? God gives us strength.
- Feeling as if you're tired and weak? God renews our soul.
- Feeling as if your needs are overwhelming? God will provide!

To endure in our faith requires us to trust God's faithfulness and love, even when dark and desperate times come. It is enough to know that~no matter what happens~God is for us.

Purpose

When our lives are falling apart or when tragedy strikes, God is with us. God never leaves us or forsakes us. It's His promise!

Practice

What difficulties are you facing? What verses in the Bible reveal God's ever-present love for you?

Prayer

Holy God, help me trust your promises and remember you are the One from whom I get my strength to endure.

Promise

I can endure all these things through the power of the one who gives me strength.

—Philippians 4:13 CEB

~ *Janet K. Johnson*

16

Unforgiveness

The Lord is close to the brokenhearted
and saves those who are crushed in spirit.

—Psalm 34:18 NIV

The story titled *The Fight to Forgive* has begun.
The beast has entered the battle.
The fight is rigged and rotten.

Unforgiveness is in the ring, boxing gloves held high, and a stench is in the air that could suck the joy out of any opponent. I decide to hold my head up and step out of the ring.

Have you battled the beast?

Several years ago, I found myself in a hard place of hearthurt. There is no timeline on the process of healing a broken heart. However, we must keep in mind there is a timeline on our life here on this earth.

It took me years. I had been hit with a bomb in the chest, but it didn't kill me.

I sat in the "pit" with clenched fists, a scowling face, and words ready to fire off if ever given the opportunity. Brokenhearted and crushed seemed to be my constant companions.

I cried out and begged God to change the offender, not to change me.

Then God reminded me of something.

We are not fighting *for* the victory; we are fighting *from* victory. The victory found in Jesus gives us strength to lay it down and walk away. We will cease saying we got the short end of the stick and instead stop carrying the stick.

Maybe the person doesn't deserve forgiveness, but do we deserve the forgiveness shown on the cross when Jesus died for us?

Life is filled with disasters of the heart, whether it be a diagnosis the Lord allows in our life, a trust issue, a rebellious child, or when a loved one of many years walks away.

We cannot have unconditional joy if we have conditional forgiveness.

Purpose

God made a big deal out of forgiveness.
I think we should too.

Practice

Who do you need to forgive?
How is holding onto unforgiveness affecting you?

Prayer

Father God, help me to forgive_____ and the
feelings I experienced because of what happened. Help
me to wipe the slate clean and to rediscover joy and
peace that surpasses all understanding. In Jesus's name
. . . amen.

Promise

Remember, the Lord forgave you,
so you must forgive others.

—Colossians 3:13b NLT

~ *Tammy Whitehurst*

17

Gratitude

Don't worry about anything; instead, pray about everything.
Tell God what you need, and thank him for all he has done.

—Philippians 4:6 NLT

"My husband is in jail," I told my friend. "I've got no money, and I'm filing for divorce. My son, Matthew, and I had to move in with my parents."

Instead of the sympathy I expected, she gave me an assignment. "I want you to make a gratitude list."

"I don't have anything to be grateful for." *Hadn't she heard what I just said?*

She started with the basics. "Do you have a roof over your head?"

"I do, but it's not *my* roof." I hadn't bought into this gratitude thing yet.

She wasn't giving up. "Do you and Matthew have food to eat? Is he healthy?"

My friend wanted me to be *grateful* in the middle of this mess. I trusted her enough to follow her instructions. At home, as I made my list, my outlook and my attitude changed.

Gratitude is an expression of faith in God and an acknowledgment of his provision. It shifts our focus from ourselves to our Creator and reminds us that He is trustworthy. He has promised to be with us. His plan and his timetable are perfect. Difficult circumstances may be beyond our control, but they are never beyond His.

When trouble comes, our minds can race with all that is wrong and how we can fix it. Finding ways to express gratitude can help us fix our eyes on Jesus and bring the peace that he offers.

Purpose

Gratitude brings peace
because it reminds us of our trust in God.

Practice

How can you find things to be grateful
for when circumstances are difficult?

Prayer

Heavenly Father, help us remember
that our help comes from you.
Show us how we can be grateful,
even in times of trouble.

Promise

Then you will experience God's peace,
which exceeds anything we can understand.
His peace will guard your hearts and minds
as you live in Christ Jesus.

—Philippians 4:7 NLT

~ *Michelle Ruddell*

18

Blessed are those who fear the Lord . . .
They will have no fear of bad news;
their hearts are steadfast, trusting in the Lord.

—Psalm 112:1, 7 NIV

We can be afraid of bad news or be steadfast and confident through it.

The path we choose reflects our willingness to trust God.

Trusting God is a choice~our stance of confidence in God's trustworthiness regardless of our circumstances!

In the middle of chronic health struggles, when I'm knocked down and discouraged, I often find myself praying for God to heal me or to change my situation. Many times, I'm not praying at all, as I'm tired and angry from the continuous hardships God has allowed.

Trials test our hearts to see whether we are willing to *trust* God, believe He is faithful and true, that He is providing hope and strength, and equipping us to endure and overcome.

Before there can be trust, there must first be a fear of the Lord. The fear of the Lord is found in our awe and reverence of His greatness, which is revealed in our delight in His Word and His ways. Our focus shifts from what we want to our great and mighty God. With our eyes on God, we must activate our faith by *choosing* to trust Him even when everything in us screams: *Turn back, don't trust, and take control!*

Activating our faith is seen in these five actions of choice:

I *am determined* to trust You, God.

I *will place* my confidence in God, who is trustworthy.

I *will surrender* to God's plan, even if that means hardship and suffering await me.

I *will remember* how God has helped me in the past, believing He will do it again.

I *will catch* every stray thought and lie, aligning it with God's truth.

With our hearts properly postured before God, we can be steadfast, trusting God with nothing to fear!

Purpose

Practicing these steps to gain an unwavering trust in God will strengthen us to face all of life's hardships!

Practice

When _____

(name your struggle),

I will _____

(activate your faith: choose one step to trust God).

Prayer

Lord, forgive me for wanting to escape the pain and struggle, rather than trust You are using even hardships for my good. Grant me an unwavering trust, a steadfastness to trust your goodness, faithfulness, and provision. Strengthen and empower me to stand so I may be immovable! Amen.

Promise

Trusting in God allows my soul to rest.

~ *Carol Fontenault*

19

Patience

But they who wait for the Lord shall renew their strength;
they shall mount up with wings like eagles;
they shall run and not be weary;
they shall walk and not faint.

—Isaiah 40:31 ESV

With our heavenly Father, patience is not passive~it requires action.

"The result of your scan shows a rare form of cancer." The doctor continued, "Surgery will be best to remove the growth." The day approached, and I did not have peace. The surgeon's office canceled and had rescheduled not just once but twice. In a state of unrest, I found myself face to the floor, surrendered. I canceled the surgery.

While I continue to wait for complete healing, I cling to the promises of the Great Physician. I am now healthier overall and growing spiritually through this trial. As I wait for His guidance, He renews my strength daily. I am content.

Waiting does not mean we do nothing, yet action does not mean we take matters into our own hands. Instead, it's an understanding that our circumstances are not always God's reality. Patience involves trusting Him and experiencing peace while we wait.

In our humanity, waiting in the middle of our struggles can be difficult. Stewarding our days to include Scripture, worship, and prayer grows our relationship with Christ and helps us walk in the Spirit. Patience is a fruit of the Holy Spirit. The more we abide in Him, the more natural it is to surrender to the process.

Purpose

Everything God does has a purpose,
and it is eternally for our good.
Patience purifies our faith;
it fosters hope and prepares us
for Christ's return.

Prompt

What actions will you take when the Holy Spirit
leads you to wait on the Lord?

Prayer

Sovereign Father, thank you for renewing my strength
as I abide in You.
I trust You with my future,
for Your promises are true.

Promise

The Lord is good to those who wait for him,
to the soul who seeks him.

—Lamentations 3:25 ESV

~ Victoria Chapin

20

Grief

I will never leave you nor forsake you.
—Hebrews 13:5 ESV

Grief is a reaction to the loss of something or someone we value and love. We all experience grief at some point during our lifetimes. It seems impossible to embrace something that hurts the heart so. So how can we fully embrace grief?

When his life support was removed, we embraced grief as our thirty-seven-year-old son Chris passed to glory. We came to grips with that this was God's plan and will for his life. We let Chris go as we listened to his heartbeat fade away into silence.

Do you think applying the little word "embrace" would cause a problem when associated with the little word "grief"? Let's ponder what Jesus did as He embraced grief at the cross.

The night before His crucifixion, Jesus prayed in the garden of Gethsemane. In agony, He began to sweat droplets of blood, crying out to Father God to let this cup pass from Him. Jesus knew His obedience would fulfill God's plan of redemption that had been established before the foundations of the world.

As followers of Jesus, we can embrace this example as a guide to live our lives. Jesus knows all the grief we will ever experience. When we place our grieving brokenness in the center of Christ, God's presence comforts us, regardless of what we have lost.

Jesus is Lord over every grieving heart. Jesus is Lord of all comfort and mercy. We can embrace grief with hope in Jesus! This hope is found in His death and resurrection. Jesus is the Lord of Life.

Purpose

Jesus is right there with us
in whatever valley we walk through.
Be assured, we can embrace our grief
that connects us to Him
in a way that we never imagined possible.

Practice

What is hurting your heart?
Is it possible for you to fully embrace
this season of grief?
What do you know about Jesus
that will guide you in this journey?

Prayer

Oh, God of heaven,
You wipe away every tear from my eyes
and embrace my heart with hope.

Promise

And we know that all things work together
for good to them that love God,
to them who are the called
according to his purpose.

—Romans 8:28 KJV

~ Nettie Patterson

21

Strength

> *The Lord is my strength and my song,*
> *and he has become my salvation.*
> *This is my God, and I will praise him,*
> *my father's God, and I will exalt him.*
>
> —Exodus 15:2 ESV

We are only as strong as our path through God's strength. The hardest time in my life when I could only survive through God's strength was the day I had to take my son off life support. Through no strength of my own, I pleaded, cried out, and begged God to show me how I could go on. There is a never-ending strength no human can explain or walk through alone. The ability to take one more breath of air, one more morning of reality, and one more step of faith comes from the all-encompassing power of God. He places people in your path and an open door you can walk through. Ironically, I didn't fully understand this since I was not a practicing Christian at the time. I reached out to Him at the lowest moment in my life.

God doesn't require you to be perfect to call out to Him for His strength to wash over you. The first step in finding true faith is reaching out to Him from the pit and watching Him lift you up.

Every day brings struggles and pain in the middle of joy and love held in both hands at the same time. God can bring you the supernatural power the world can never show you.

Purpose

When you rely and trust on His strength and love,
you can make it another day through all
life brings you.

Practice

How can you draw closer to God's strength
when life seems impossible on your own?

Prayer

Father God, Your strength is sufficient in my life
when I am hopeless.

Promise

Love the Lord your God with all your heart
and with all your soul and with all your might.

—Deuteronomy 6:5 ESV

~ *Phylis Mantelli*

22

Be still in the presence of the Lord
and wait patiently for him to act.
—Psalm 37:7 NLT

What does it mean to *be still* in the presence of the Lord? Standing in my backyard on a sunny fall afternoon, I raised my eyes to the heavens and shouted, "WHY DON'T YOU ANSWER ME?"

My son had died eleven months before, and I had not heard the quiet voice of the Holy Spirit since his death. I was weary with grief and desperate for answers.

My racing mind knew no rest. I wandered about the yard raking leaves with a lack of purpose, weeping with every step.

In that moment, He spoke to me in my spirit and took me to His Word.

Being still before the Lord means resting on the knowledge of God and trusting His heart of compassion. It's waiting for His help in a spirit of confidence.

In our deepest despair we look anxiously for God to do something because we desire an answer. We cry out in the deepest parts of our being, "Please, God, do something." Just because we don't hear His voice or see the answer to our prayers doesn't mean He's not listening and working out all things for our good.

Purpose

Resting on his unchanging Word,
waiting with anticipation, and believing with
confidence that He is who He says He is leads us to
know He will do what He says He will do.
Then being still in the presence of the Lord is
no longer a challenge but a relief.

Practice

What is keeping you from being still in
His presence?

Prayer

Lord, show me Your heart through Your Word and
help me be still with confidence in Your presence.

Promise

Never will I leave you; never will I forsake you.

—Hebrews 13:5b NIV

~ Teresa Davis

23

Let the word of Christ dwell in you richly in all wisdom,
teaching and admonishing one another in psalms, hymns,
and spiritual songs, singing with grace in your hearts to the
Lord.

—Colossians 3:16 NKJV

When God's Word is at home in your heart, there is no room for worry.

Have you ever experienced heart-pounding pressure building up on the inside when you begin to worry and fret over a difficult situation that shows up knocking on your door?

When I find myself here, I remember what Ruth Graham, wife of evangelist Billy Graham, said, "Quit studying the problems and start studying the promises." This is a helpful reminder to me when facing problems I cannot control or fix on my own.

The word "dwell" in Colossians 3:16 is a compound word which means "to dwell in a house." The last part of the verse mentions psalms, hymns, and spiritual songs.

As we let the Word of Christ dwell in us richly, we are allowing the God-breathed, living and active, Spirit-filled Word to make its home in our hearts. Not just as an occasional guest but a permanent resident with full access to every room in our house.

I have discovered the easiest way to throw down the welcome mat and allow God's Word to dwell in my heart is through memorizing it by putting the Scriptures to music. I use my phone to record whatever tune I create for the Scripture. Then I listen to my recording over and over throughout the day and continue to do this until it dwells in my heart permanently. The Scriptures then become like background music playing in mind, reminding me of the truths in God's Word.

Purpose

When we invite Christ through His Word to dwell in
our heart
by daily reading, meditating, and memorizing it,
we open the door to experience the riches
of the hidden treasures found only there.

Practice

In what area have you been studying on your problem
instead of dwelling on the promises of God?
What can you do to bring the truths
of His Word to mind?

Prayer

Lord, forgive me for allowing anxiety and worry
to have any access in my heart.
Help me to welcome your Word in my heart daily,
filling every room with songs of praise.

Promise

He who dwells in the secret place of the Most High
shall abide under the shadow of the Almighty.

—Psalm 91:1 NKJV

~ Teresa Harmening

23

*This means that anyone who belongs to Christ
has become a new person. The old life is gone; a new life
has begun!*

—2 Corinthians 5:17 NLT

Who are you? Why are you here?

I found myself asking these questions and more. Most importantly, I asked, "What purpose would God have for someone like me?" I knew who I thought I was~an overweight, unworthy, unwanted wife and mother of two with a shameful past. This was the lie I had allowed the enemy to use to imprison me.

But as redeemed believers in Christ, we have a new identity, and the old one is gone (2 Cor. 5:17). However, until we embrace this truth and learn to live forgiven, we will never feel as if we are worthy enough for God's purposes. Forgiving ourselves for past mistakes can feel impossible. We need the Lord's help, and we can only find it in His Word.

Speaking truth over your life will refresh your mind and restore your soul. But to speak the truth, we must know what it is, so reading His Word daily is imperative. Jesus used the Word of God to rebuke Satan, and it is the only weapon we possess to fight our spiritual battles. However, like any fine weapon, it must be sharp to be effective.

Purpose

When the enemy tries to bind us with lies,
we find truth in the holy Word of God.

Practice

What are the lies Satan uses to imprison you? What
truth from His Word will set you free?

Prayer

Lord, help me break free from the enemy's lies and
embrace the truth of who I am through
Jesus Christ.

Promise

And you will know the truth,
and the truth will set you free.

—John 8:32 NLT

~ Tracey Glenn

25

For the LORD is good and his love endures forever;
his faithfulness continues through all generations.

—Psalm 100:5 NIV

I immediately knew the clunky white cardboard glasses to view the movie were *not* intended to make a fashion statement. The "magic" glasses drew the audience into a three-dimensional view that brought the screen alive. We dodged critters and monsters that jumped out at us as we leaned left and right on simulated vehicle rides.

However, when the *real* monsters of life attack, we need more than a pair of glasses to focus *and* survive.

Having dealt with death, divorce, and disease, I describe my journey as "Life in 3D." Each event brought disappointment, discouragement, and desperation. I yearned for stability in my somersaulting world. In my brokenness, I cried out to God and discovered a personal relationship with the 3D Creator of the universe~the Father, Son, and Holy Spirit.

When the monsters of life jump out at you, how do you respond? Do you focus on yourself and your impossible circumstances or on God and His possibilities?

When we humbly acknowledge our need for our faithful God, He comes alongside with His presence to comfort and guide us. He uses our challenges to help define our identity, discover our purpose, and develop our discipleship.

Just as God brought deep healing to my broken places, you, too, can find hope and joy by personalizing His promises:

God loves *me* (Jer. 31:3).

God is with *me* always (Ps. 139:7–10).

God makes *all* things new (2 Cor. 5:17).

Purpose

Personalize the promises of God in your own life.

Practice

Do you find yourself focusing on yourself and your impossible circumstances or on God and His possibilities? Think of a specific example for each.

Prayer

Thank you, faithful God, that you long to fill me with the unlimited height, width, length, and depth of your love. Help me to humbly receive the precious gifts you want to entrust to me. In Jesus's name. Amen.

Promise

Neither death nor life, neither angels nor demons, neither the present nor the future, nor any powers, neither height nor depth, nor anything else in all creation, will be able to separate us from the love of God that is in Christ Jesus our Lord.

—Romans 8:38–39 NIV

~ *Linda Y. Hammond*

26

My peace I give you . . . do not be afraid.
—John 14:27 NIV

Ever felt like a bottle cork on wash cycle?

I have~the day we got caught in a storm on the North Sea.

Our four-man sailboat captained by our Dutch friend Maarten ventured farther and farther out to sea until we could no longer see land.

When I looked at the blackening sky, the angry waves, and the impossible circumstances, I was terrified. Then I looked at Maarten. He was grinning from ear to ear.

"Wow! Isn't this great!" he hollered over the roar of the waves as they carried our tiny boat skyward.

I switched my focus from the sky, the waves, and the water-filled boat and fixed my gaze on Maarten, the one with the controls in the palm of his hand and a gleam in the center of his eye. When I took my eyes off Maarten and focused on the violent storm, I'd panic. So my eyes became riveted on Maarten's grin, and I found peace . . . because the one who was in control was at peace.

Friend, you may be struggling to keep your head above water while the winds of adversity whirl you around. Where is your gaze? Backward at the pain of your past? Inward at the relentless hurt? Outward at the hopeless circumstances? Or upward at the One who can give you peace amid your storms?

Peace comes when we focus on the God of all peace~ trusting Him to see us through our storm.

Purpose

When we fix our eyes on God, not our problems,
and pray expectantly for wisdom and direction
from the only One who is truly in control~
we can find peace.

Practice

What storm of life are you focusing on?
What would God's peace mean to you?

Prayer

Lord, help me keep my focus on You and be thankful
for my storm along with Your peace during it.

Promise

You will keep in perfect peace all who trust in you,
all whose thoughts are fixed on you!

—Isaiah 26:3 NLT

~ *Sandi Banks*

27

Confidence

Let us hold tightly without wavering to the hope we affirm,
for God can be trusted to keep his promise.
—Hebrews 10:23 NLT

The definition of confidence can be confusing. Frequently, we substitute the world's definition for the biblical definition. A worldly confidence is an appreciation of our abilities or qualities; however, biblical confidence is the belief and understanding that we can rely on God—a firm trust.

I had become confident in navigating a chronic illness, rheumatoid arthritis, and its pain and crippling effects. Defying most medical diagnoses, I had a false security, believing I could defeat any illness.

I once said to a friend, "I don't ever worry about other diseases, including cancer, because what are the odds that I would have two diseases? Surely, God agrees with me."

My friend, a medical professional, gasped and said, "That is not true."

My misguided medical understanding and God's Word were about to collide. Counting the odds is not biblical and is arrogant, while trusting God with all results regardless of our diagnosis or circumstance is. The truth is we can be given multiple diagnoses, but only God gives the prognosis.

Navigating my own life with rheumatoid arthritis did not give me any firm trust on the day I was diagnosed with cancer and given ninety days to live. I immediately called out to God, recognizing my past medical experience would not solve this dilemma. Confidence, a firm trust in God, is what conquers fear and hopelessness. Today, my ninety days is twenty years.

God's children face the same day-in, day-out circumstance as others; however, we are not reliant on ourselves for answers or solutions to our circumstances.

Purpose

We are confident if we approach the throne of God
we will find mercy and grace to help us
in our time of need.

Practice

Where is your confidence?
Is it in something other than God?
If so, refocus and approach His throne,
confessing your lack of confidence.

Prayer

Lord, help me let go of any worldly confidence
and remain confident in You alone.

Promise

So let us come boldly
to the throne of our gracious God.
There we will receive his mercy,
and we will find grace to help us
when we need it most.

—Hebrews 4:16 NLT

~ *Cherie Nettles*

28

Holy

*"Give the following instructions
to the entire community of Israel.
You must be holy because I,
the Lord your God, am holy."*

—Leviticus 19:2 NLT

When was the last time you described yourself as holy? Is it on your resume or social media bio?

At first glance, the only thing I could consider holy about myself is a pair of jeans and maybe a few socks! That is, until I looked deeper.

Isaiah describes seraphim flying around the throne of God crying out, "Holy, holy, holy is the Lord of Heaven's Armies!

The whole earth is filled with his glory" (Isa. 6:3 NLT). We sing "holy" to praise God in new worship songs and old hymns. God deserves it! He is set apart, sacred, and worthy of complete devotion.

We don't usually think of ourselves as holy. What does that even mean in relation to humanity?

The Greek word *hagios* is used 235 times in the New Testament. It is a form of holy that means: "to set apart, saintly." It indicates devotion to, and doing the work of, a deity.

Is God asking us to be perfect? Of course not! He is acknowledging that we are a chosen people and desires the surrender of our lives. We are to live each day as a reflection of His Son, Jesus.

Purpose

The good news is we are called holy even while
exceptionally flawed!

Practice

In what ways are you set apart in your community?
Are you charitable? Are the fruits of the spirit
flourishing in you and recognizable to others? Today,
write down three ways that your actions reflect
holiness.

Prayer

Lord, help me to believe in holiness as my identity
and put it into action. Cleanse me of unrighteousness
in order that I may bring you glory. In Jesus's name,
amen.

Promise

For God's will was for us to be made holy
by the sacrifice of the body of Jesus Christ,
once for all time.

—Hebrews 10:10 NLT

~ *Andrea O. Smith*

29

Believe

Now faith is confidence in what we hope for
and assurance about what we do not see.

—Hebrews 11:1 NIV

Do you believe in God, or do you believe God?

When our faith is rooted in God's actions, it's not faith at all. This type of faith demonstrates we are not believing God; instead we merely believe in what God does.

The journey of Moses throughout the exodus is littered with miracles. An astonishing rescue of a baby from the Nile, the awesome appearance of the Lord in a burning bush, the astounding parting of the sea, and the amazing provision of daily food rained down from heaven.

Each instance in this narrative surely should have produced great faith, and yet the people doubted throughout their wilderness experience.

Even Moses is not just credited for his faith found in these events. In Hebrews 11:27 (NIV) the text clearly says, "By faith . . . he persevered because he saw him who is invisible."

Seeing God for who He is and not what He does produces a faith that is deeply rooted in His character. It is this kind of faith that withstands trials even when the raging sea does not part and bring rescue. Real faith can say with assurance, "I believe," even when my prayers aren't answered according to my plan.

Daily life brings us circumstances that test our faith: a wayward child, an unexpected diagnosis, infidelity, financial ruin, disastrous decisions, and destructive relationships. Yet, through it all, when our eyes see the One who is invisible, we can withstand each situation.

Purpose

When we don't know what God is doing,
we can still believe, resting
in the truth of who He is!

Practice

What circumstance is testing your belief?
What attributes of your God can meet you there?

Prayer

Lord, give me faith to believe,
not simply in your activity,
but a faith tethered to Your identity.
Help me believe You, God!

Promise

May the God of hope
fill you with all joy and peace as you trust in Him,
so that you may overflow with hope
by the power of the Holy Spirit.

—Romans 15:13 NIV

~ *Carol Tetzlaff*

30

Expectation

*Now as the people were in expectation, and all reasoned in
their hearts about John, whether he was the Christ or not,
John answered, saying to all, "I indeed baptize you with
water; but One mightier than I is coming, whose sandal
strap I am not worthy to loose . . ."*

—Luke 3:15–16 NKJV

When a woman learns she's expecting a baby, suddenly her
perspective changes. All aspects of life take on an entirely
new hue as her thoughts about the future change. Her
habits change. Her view of finances and even the words she
speaks change.

Prior to the passage in Luke 3:15–16, God had been silent
for 400 years. No prophets. No word from God. Just deafening

silence. And then suddenly, John the Baptist bursts onto the scene, and the people were in expectation, anticipating the coming Messiah.

As it was for them, so it should be for us! With the political and cultural climate today, this is not the time to give in to fear, despair, and panic. This is the time to stand and look up in expectation for a mighty move of the Spirit of God in our homes, our churches, our towns, and the nations.

Oh, the power of holy expectation! Everything changes when we are expecting. Look up in expectation!

May we live in daily expectation where everything changes:
The way we pray~greater faith.
The way we worship~a way of life.
The way we linger in His presence~a longing for Him.
The way we love others~whether we are loved in return.
The way we walk through suffering~trusting Him in our pain.

Practice

Are you living a life of expectation? In what specific places do you find yourself longing for Jesus?

Prayer

Lord, may I live in daily expectation of seeing you, hearing you, knowing you, and being loved by you.

Promise

My soul, wait silently for God alone, for my expectation is from Him.

—Psalm 62:5 NKJV

~ Shelly Brown

and the Christian Communicators Conference

*A*fter reading this devotional, do you feel a tug on your heart to tell your story? Perhaps you want to write a book or share a message from the stage.

We at Redemption Press have partnered together with the Christian Communicators Conference to provide the tools, training, and guidance to share your message.

Our team at Redemption Press would love to talk with you to explore how we can help you write your story. Our team is ready to walk with you through every step of the publishing process from idea to launch. Contact us at Redemption-Press. com.

The Christian Communicators Conference is a place where you can learn how to share your message from the stage with excellence and confidence. See how you can join this incredible group of speakers at christiancommunicators.com.

Maybe next time you will find your words on the pages of this devotional!

Meet the Authors

The authors found in this devotional all have a passion to bring a message of hope and are available to speak. You can learn more about them by visiting their websites or contacting them by email. All these women are certified speakers under Christian Communicators.

Sandi Banks is an author, speaker, and devotional workshop leader who draws inspiration from her adventures through forty countries, and forty-plus years of life as a wife, mom, and Gramma to some amazing folks (sandibanks.com).

Lori Boruff loves Midwest lake life with her husband, Rick. As a trusted life coach, speaker, writer, and Christian Communicator co-director, Lori offers transformational tools for healing and hope (loriboruff.com).

Shelly Brown co-leads hybrid publishing company Redemption Press. She serves with Love UnVeiled, a transformational discipleship ministry that helps women experience healing, transformation, and freedom. Shelly lives in Orlando, Florida, where her favorite role is grandma to three beautiful grandgirls (shelly@redemption-press.com).

Victoria Chapin is a speaker, chaplain, and author as well as a wife, mom, and grammy whose ministry inspires people to find jewels in adversity and victory in Jesus. She loves everything coffee, especially when shared with friends (victoriachapin.com).

Teresa Davis is a grief mentor, author, speaker, and podcaster. An encourager by design who has helped many on their journey toward healing, Teresa is a wife of thirty-nine years, mother of two, and Nana to five grandbabies. She and her family live in southern Indiana just across the river from Louisville, Kentucky~home of the Kentucky Derby (thegriefmentor.com).

Christina England was labeled "super-morbidly obese" for over twenty years. From a pit of desperation, she asked God to step in, and he transformed her from the inside out. She is a speaker, author, and worship leader (christinaengland.com).

Carol Fontenault is a speaker, author, and pastoral counselor and an engaging and compelling voice inspiring women to walk closely with their God! Learn more about encountering God at carolfontenault.com.

Tracey Glenn is ranch-raised and Jesus saved. Her life has been a wild ride from horse trainer to business owner. Author of *Gathering the Wayward Heart*, Tracey gives God the glory (brandedinfaith.com).

Linda Hammond, forgiven Christ-follower, wife, mother, grandmother, writer, and speaker, encourages the broken-hearted to experience renewal through Jesus Christ. Formerly a senior pastor's administrative assistant for thirty-four years, she now coleads the Christian Writers Workshop in Waco, Texas (lyhammond86@gmail.com).

Teresa Harmening is a speaker, worship leader, and songwriter and is currently writing a book. She encourages women to dig deeper into the Word and discover the joy of using their God-given gifts (teresaharmening.com).

Cristi Helin is a speaker, blogger, and host of her podcast *Soar to Joy*. Her testimony encourages women to trust God's character and to believe He will get us through, if we don't quit (cristihelin@protonmail.com).

Athena Dean Holtz is founder and publisher of Redemption Press and the *She Writes for Him* community of writers. She is always excited to share stories of God's faithfulness, especially in her memoir, *Full Circle: Coming Home to the Faithfulness of God* (athenadeanholtz.com).

Janet K. Johnson is an award-winning author and speaker whose life losses led her to seek God more deeply. Moving from grief to true inner joy, she brings hope and God's promises to her audiences. Connect with her at janetkjohnson.com.

Carol Kent is the executive director of Speak Up Ministries. Carol's books have sold over one million copies. She founded the Speak Up Conference, with speaking and writing tracks. She has been a speaker at Women of Faith, Extraordinary Women, and Women of Joy arena events (carolkent.org).

Kris Howsley King is an author and speaker, wife to Randy, mom to three married children, and Kooki to eight grands who loves God's Word, Cheetos, and office supplies. Fun-finder and joy-seeker, she loves helping others find their purpose (krishowsleyking.com).

Robin Luftig is an author and national speaker addressing healing after tragedy who says, "Be grateful in everything~even the bumpy rides!" (robinluftig.com).

Phylis Mantelli is a speaker and author of the book *Unmothered: Life with a Mom Who Couldn't Love Me* (phylismantelli.com).

Dr. Mary Miner enjoys physical activity, time with her husband and soon-to-be child, and helping others from her own experiences in walking with Jesus (dogoodonlylife.com).

Pam Mitchael is a writer, speaker, and Bible teacher whose testimony of redemption and restoration is a reminder that no pain, rejection, or shame is wasted when fully surrendered to God (pammitchael.com).

Cherie Nettles is a comedienne and speaker who believes laughter is the best medicine. Married with two grown children, her baby is Clarence, a yorkie-poo, purchased half-off (cherienettle.net).

Nettie Patterson is the worship leader at her church in Bullard, Texas. She loves to sing, speak, and write for the Lord. Nettie lives on a farm with her husband in Troup, Texas (nettiepatterson.com).

Susie Roberts enjoys teaching women how to find healing for their wounded hearts. She believes her healing began when she started believing who God says she is (susanlouiseroberts@hotmail.com).

Na'Kedra Rodgers is a speaker and author. A southern belle with sass, she knows both heartache and hope and is an encourager who spreads optimism using biblically-based, uplifting speeches~ "OptimisticallyKe . . . that's me" (okthatsme.com)!

Michelle Ruddell is a Central Texas speaker, author, and teacher. After the loss of her five-year-old-son, Matthew, in a car accident, she learned joy and sorrow can coexist (michelleruddell.com).

Andrea O. Smith is a speaker, author, wife, homeschool mom of four, and silver-linings hunter. Creator of *God Met Me in a Moment*, she celebrates finding God in life's messes and miracles (andreaosmith.com).

Cheri Strange is wife of Chad and mom to eight, a *YouVersion* content partner, the author of *Can You See Me, Now*, and *Life Principles for Living the Greatest Commandment* (sheryearns. com).

Carol Tetzlaff is an author, speaker, and co-owner of Redemption Press. She loves all things yellow, supersweet icedcoffee, and living in Arizona with her husband and family "forest" that includes eleven grandkiddos. She is the author of *Ezra: Unleashing the Power of Praise, a 7-week Bible Study* (caroltetzlaff.com).

Lori Vober suffered a stroke at age twenty-nine. She is a walking miracle and feels called to share her journey of faith and perseverance to encourage others. Connect with her at www. lorivober.com.

Joy Wendling is a parent coach, speaker, and writer. She encourages parents to be more peaceful, purposeful, and playful on her podcast, *Playfully Faithful Parenting* (createdtoplay.com).

Tammy Whitehurst is a full-time motivational speaker. She is the codirector of the Christian Communicators Conference. Find out more about her at TammyWhitehurst.com.

This devotional is a compilation of writings from authors and speakers from the Christian Communicators Conference 2022. To order please go to redemption-press.com or wherever books are sold.

ORDER INFORMATION

REDEMPTION
P R E S S

To order additional copies of this book, please visit
www.redemption-press.com.
Also available at Christian bookstores and wherever books are sold.

CPSIA information can be obtained
at www.ICGtesting.com
Printed in the USA
BVHW041515260623
666388BV00001B/3

9 781951 350185